Path

The Art of Organizing Uncertainty

Jack Ricchiuto

Nuance Works

Books by Jack Ricchiuto

Collaborative Creativity / 1996
Accidental Conversations / 2002
Project Zen / 2003
Appreciative Leadership / 2005
Mountain Paths / 2007
Conscious Becoming / 2008
Instructions From The Cook / 2009
The Stories That Connect Us / 2010
Enchantment Of Casual Origins / 2011
The Joy Of Thriving / 2012
Ordinary Eyes / 2012
The Agile Canvas Field Guide / 2012
Abundant Possibilities / 2013
The Power Of Circles / 2013
Making Sense Of Time / 2014
Beyond Recipes / 2014
Focus / 2015
Smarter Together / 2015
Ideas / 2015
The Art Of Conversations / 2016
The Way Of Questions / 2017
The Growth Imperative / 2018
Simple Listening / 2019
Path / 2019

3 | Path

Path

The art of organizing uncertainty

Jack Ricchiuto

Nuance Works

1020 Kenilworth Avenue

Cleveland OH 44113 USA

NuanceWorks.com

ISBN 9781096647959

Paperback

I. Title

1. Planning. Goal setting. Personal growth.
   Organizational development. Project
   management.

First edition, September 2019

Printed in the USA

Production: Kindle Direct Publishing

Cover: Tia Andrako

Forward: Douglas Craver

Contents

For a complementary copy of *A Path Method Guide*, a step by step guide to the process, email Jack@NuanceWorks.com

Forward

Think of the happiness discovered in being mindfully equipped to pursue your personal interests and those of others without the limitations of goals and plans.

Lifting the limitations of expectations in favor of the power of questions. Using questions to organize and overcome what you perceive as uncertainty. You are about to turn the pages of a book I know breaks new ground in the optimization and sustainability of work in our personal and professional lives.

I feel like I should know this book after countless discussions with Jack about the questions, ideas, and topics that lay the foundation of Path.

Yet even after those personal interactions, especially those driven by the wind and water as we sail Passage this Summer on Sandusky Bay, and reading several drafts, I learn

something new about myself each time I read
and discuss it.

As a result of that learning, I ask increasingly
better path questions of myself and others that
allow the possibilities before us to unfold.

Today we live in a world where solutions to
problems are increasingly difficult to discover
because human nature still clings to the myth
that answers are black and white. The black and
white of right vs. wrong. We want to believe
some people are more gifted at getting it right,
and some are burdened with getting it wrong.

This myth is clung to because we seek the
comfort of a false sense of security against the
anxiety of the gray found between black and
white. If you're honest with yourself, you know
exactly what I'm referring to here.

At one time or another, we've all gotten caught
in this destructive loop, loop after loop, and felt
the deep disappointment of failure only to
repeat it again. Or worse yet, we don't get far
enough to know whether we'll succeed or fail

because our goals and plans act as a drag on momentum even as we seek the satisfaction of checking things off our checklist. We cling to deadlines, afraid to let go, in order to make us feel like the end of our work is in sight, only to learn we are blinded by the assumptions we make.

What if we could learn the construct of a new method and practice that allows us to overcome the limitations of this thought process (or the lack thereof), and scale the possibilities before us that give life its meaning?

A method and practice that equips us with the necessary fluidity around rocks of the unknown, instead of against, like water flowing through a river. A new language, if you will, that turns uncertainty into magic.

Path: The Art of Organizing Uncertainty teaches this new language. A language just like Jack's writing and work -- where there is never a wasted word. I challenge you, as I've challenged myself, to become fluent in this method and practice with its liberating velocity of opportunity and path questions that facilitate an infinite possibility space where there is no failure, only feedback. The type of feedback that grows in value with each experiment.

In the words of Annie Dillard, "How we spend our days is, of course, how we spend our lives."

A path method and practice have become and will continue to be the catalyst of my limitless possibilities and those of the startup founders and teams I coach, day in, day out.

I invite you to join me in this innovating, stimulating, and rewarding work to move beyond the limitations of goals and plans.

Namaste.

Douglas Craver
Founder and Coach
StartupBuilder.Life

Invitation

We live in a world where we have access to more information in a day than anyone a few generations ago had in a year. This reality has unprecedented impacts on our relationship to the future.

It is perhaps no coincidence, nor greater paradox, that the more information we have access to, the more uncertainty we experience.

For all our predictive optimism or cynicism, the future remains curiously unknowable. As certain as we might be about at least knowing ourselves, we can't even predict our next twenty thoughts. Being adaptive has become the new normal.

There is a profound correlation between how much we enjoy our life and our relationship to uncertainty. Our capacity to enjoy life is equal to our capacity to view uncertainty as an endless, magnificent opportunity space.

Uncertainty is the most fertile space of exploration and creativity we will ever know. Tapping into its immense power is simply a matter of translating it into paths of inspiring and productive questions.

The dialogue here is a shared exploration into how we can make uncertainty more magical than we ever imagined.

Jack Ricchiuto
September 2019

Uncertainty

The fabric of life is woven from two strands, certainty, and uncertainty. These strands are strands of language.

Certainty is the language of prediction, assumption, and expectation. Uncertainty is the language of unknowns, curiosity, and questions.

Uncertainty is the experience of things being unclear, things going not as planned, things unfolding unpredictably. For most of us, uncertainty is more everyday than rare.

In our better moments, we ponder these spaces of uncertainty the way creative souls approach fresh canvases, blank pages, quiet kitchens, silent instruments, and empty stages.

Uncertainty punctuates the vocabulary of an otherwise predictable life with unpredictable challenges, changes, passions and projects.

A loved one has a setback. They announce a change at work. We're not all getting along at work. A friend is in crisis. Our partner is going through a rough patch. We want to finally do what we have for too long put off.

We start a new job, love, family, adventure. Our life is turned upside down in the loss of someone or something of significance. We close a chapter in our life. We find ourselves at the next crossroads.

Uncertainty can span moments, hours, days, weeks, months, even years. It's messy. Our landscapes exceed our maps.

In uncertainty, setting measurable goals and making detailed plans doesn't feel realistic. There are too many unknowns to commit to anything definitive.

We don't decide when uncertainty starts or completes. No matter how much predictability we try to engineer into our life, uncertainty remains life's signature.

We've been organizing uncertainty since we were young. Everything we have ever achieved and survived came about because we made transitions from uncertainty to clarity. We can't avoid uncertainty, but we can organize and flourish in it.

The conversation here is how organizing uncertainty can be intentionally possible, in any context, at any scale.

What you're describing in taking on possibilities, projects, and challenges often does feel like uncertainty. But uncertainty seems so random.

Interestingly, there is science to it. In chaos theory, we discover that there is nothing random in nature. There are always unseen patterns in what might appear random. Not seeing patterns is not evidence none exist.

Social insects are prime examples. With literally no goals, plans, or bosses, there are definite, intelligent, and productive patterns in the swarming of ants and bees.

Reflecting on times when we went from uncertainty to something productive, we made sense of the chaos, and from this sense, made good things possible.

Uncertainty doesn't mean unmanageable disorder. It is an opportunity space. There is a hidden order of questions in the swirling of things we don't know. The reason we ever have new opportunities is precisely because of life's intrinsic uncertainty.

Is it human nature to have a bias for predictability?

Our brains are hardwired for predictability. We delight in the familiar and similar. We like things that makes sense. We are comforted by knowing what to expect. Our emotions have gravitational pull because they are predictions.

Routines and habits create, restore, and sustain a sense of predictability. Addictions can serve a similar purpose.

Having a sense of predictability doesn't make organizing uncertainty more or less possible.

Is there an easy way to identify where uncertainty happens in our lives?

We can start with the contrast of where uncertainty might not be.

What's already on our calendars? What are our regular daily and weekly routines? What and whom do we feel like we can count on? What are our most important commitments and obligations? What seems to going well and as expected?

These are the pockets of predictability in our life. The rest is some version of uncertainty.

Even though some people can present the illusion of a fairly perfect life, there is not one of us 7.5 billion people on the planet who doesn't have some kind of uncertainty. It's intrinsic to the human condition.

In our most honest moments with ourselves, we admit the future is largely unknowable. In our more wobbly moments, we don't mind uncertainty, as long as it doesn't happen to us.

Some people seem to flourish in the unfamiliar. What's their story?

Even as they enjoy moments of predictability as much as anyone, there are those who love the new and unpredictable. They relish being creative and being around creative people and things. They like spaces beyond careful.

They love to read and travel widely. They come alive in accidental conversations with strangers. They like discovering new cultures and cuisines. They prefer what excites their curiosity and imagination.

People who love unpredictability see new challenges and opportunities as gifts, open spaces of new possibilities. They love learning, discovering, trying new things.

Uncertainty doesn't send them into self-protection. It sends them into self-expansion.

How does our relationship to uncertainty factor into our need for control?

Some of us seem to need more control than others. To the extent uncertainty is an unwelcome source of discomfort, we feel a need to control all manner of things in our life and our world.

We feel a need to control our feelings and the feelings of others. We feel a need to control the conditions, dynamics, and events around us. Success is measured in units of certainty.

As much as we feel a need to control other people and things, we are sensitive and resistant to being controlled. Feeling controlled puts us out of control. We also resist taking more responsibility than we need because that can be a hot mess of uncertainty.

Ironically, a felt need for control stirs up and sustains cycles of uncertainty for ourselves and others. The more control we think we need, the more we try controlling things, the more uncertainty we have, which leads to more need for control. The need for control diminishes as we discover how to organize uncertainty.

Are there disadvantages to having a strong preference for predictability?

We make life more difficult and complicated than it needs to be when we make certainty a condition for our ability to grow and flourish.

No matter how many goals we set and plans we make, uncertainty in all its forms and on all its scales will continue to be a constant.

Until we make friends with uncertainty, we feel uneasy in our world and uncomfortable in our own skin. Feeling at home in our world and at peace within ourselves means being friends with uncertainty.

When unpredictability is no longer a constraint, we experience a creative sense of freedom to make our life as interesting as we want it to be.

So, moments of uncertainty can be a source of delight or distress.

Uncertainty holds no intrinsic feeling. In its natural, dynamic state, uncertainty can provoke anxiety, frustration, or loneliness. It can also evoke interest, curiosity, and connection.

Uncertainty is a structural rather than emotional reality. Uncertainty can provoke and evoke feelings, but is not itself a feeling.

Which end of the emotional continuum we relate from depends on whether we see uncertainty as a problem to avoid or gift to engage.

It is an ancient and enduring truth in human experience that trying to resist, avoid, or prevent uncertainty creates suffering. We create unnecessary suffering and fragility in our life, work, and relationships by trying to uncertainty-proof our life.

Uncertainty is the human condition. It is a potential source of humility, wholeness, and integrity. It happens regardless of economic status, education, gender, generation, or geography.

How do we learn to make uncertainty a problem to prevent rather than gift to engage?

Our relationship to uncertainty is significantly shaped by the language of our socialization. We listen to how the language we hear reveals attitudes toward uncertainty.

We hear our parents, families, teachers, and friends love and loath the unplanned. We notice how their language reveals a bias for curiosity and certainty.

For reasons not always clear, we resonate more with certain significant others. We take on the language of these we naturally resonate with.

Throughout our life, we gravitate toward people who think and speak the same kind of language we think and speak in. We form and join tribes of perspectives we find most familiar to ours.

How does traditional education factor into this? Isn't education supposed to help us become more adaptable to the speed of change and uncertainty?

When educational success is measured in units of tested memorization, it diminishes curiosity. Without curiosity, uncertainty is stressful.

Year by year, students temporarily lose their capacity for curiosity as they develop an addiction to certainty. We teach them that success is more about having the right answers than the right questions.

When promotions and graduations go to those who have more answers than questions, it makes uncertainty an untenable and uncomfortable cause of failure.

The years of our greatest brain and mind growth are those where uncertainty is an endless beach of exploration and creativity. This growth slows as we learn to view unclarity as the enemy to overcome rather than a friend to play with along the way.

Formal education can be maladaptive, causing us to be less adaptable when it rewards answers rather than questions. Only curiosity has the power to support and grow our capacity for adaptability.

Can we learn to see uncertainty as an opportunity space?

Because our brains have no permanent structures, we can, at any time in our life, learn to have a different relationship to uncertainty.

Our brains have no intrinsic attachment to certainty. Nor do they have an inevitable discomfort with uncertainty. Any of us can cultivate the ability to flourish in everyday uncertainty.

When we grow a more open and engaged relationship to uncertainty, we find ourselves living a more interesting life.

We live with a greater sense of contribution and purpose, meaning and courage, creativity and adaptability.

What about goals and plans? They seem like common sense ways to prevent and manage uncertainty.

We have been socialized to assume goals and plans have the ability to manage and prevent uncertainty.

As good as they might look on paper, goals and plans can fail 92% of the time. This is true in personal, professional, and public contexts.

The origin of the word goal is about limits and boundaries. Goals fail for two reasons: they make us unrealistic and mindless.

They are unrealistic because they are based on the assumptions of opinions, speculations, and worries. We take action on a static version of reality we assume will exist. We're supposed to feel good about our assumptions, but as long as life keeps reminding us about its constant of change, we don't.

Acting on assumptions is the most effective way to cause all kinds of doubts, missteps, and delays that add additional layers of unnecessary uncertainty to the uncertainty we already have.

If we find ourselves suffering from an uncertainty deficiency, recovery can be as simple as setting some goals or making some plans.

Mindlessness is not noticing what's new in our world. The more we stay busy trying to prove our assumptions right, the more we miss noticing the continuous churn of new possibilities. Without mindful creativity and adaptability, we sustain the uncertainty.

There is nothing intrinsically wrong with goals and plans. They can express our most significant priorities and promises. They just don't have the power to organize uncertainty. Organizing uncertainty takes being entirely realistic and mindful.

The practical utility of goals and plans is how their abundance of assumptions can be leveraged to form the kinds of questions that have the power to organize uncertainty.

Don't we have to have assumptions about the future to create it? How could we possibly move forward without the assumptions of opinions, speculations, and expectations?

One of the things our brains are good at is manufacturing the assumptions of opinions, speculations, and expectations.

Our brains excel in this especially in moments of uncertainty.

Even though we've been socialized to believe assumptions are crucial to success, there is no evidence for it. If anything, the evidence suggests otherwise.

Boeing Built Deadly Assumptions Into 737 Max, Blind to a Late Design Change. This was a recent headline on the flight disasters plaguing this engineering giant. Companies of their caliber would be considered the epitome of the best, most heavily certified and regulated goal and planning practices.

The seduction of goals and plans is the illusion of predictability they create through their undertows of assumptions. Despite how perfect we try to get our goals and plans , assumptions create the illusion of predictability but not the reality of it.

Assumptions keep us busy. Busyness creates the appearance of productivity and progress. As long as our assumptions disregard the constant of change, they don't move us forward.

Our disappointment in the durability of goals and the promise of plans is not a function of our personal or collective incompetence. It is the inherent and unintended design flaw of assumption-based goals and plans.

It would be lovely if goals and plans lived up to their hype. When we want to know what is likely to not happen in times of uncertainty, all we need to do is look at our assumptions.

What do these have in common: Polaroid, Kodak, Sears, Yahoo, MySpace, and IBM?

Aside from all having once achieved rock star status, and having been ruled by well educated and paid people, the assumptions of their goals and plans led to missed opportunities while others learned their way into disruptive futures.

NASA once calculated that on their most complex and successful space missions, they were "off plan" around 90% of the time. Their success was not dependent on staying faithful to their plans. Their success was testament to their favoring constant curiosity over assumptions.

These stories are calls for reimagining how we organize uncertainty. It's an invitation to invent and learn radically new and alternative models.

If organizing uncertainty isn't about goals and plans, what is it about?

Organizing uncertainty is about a shift in language. Our language makes us realistic or unrealistic, mindful or mindless. The implications are profound.

To organize uncertainty, we don't need a different reality. We don't need a different personality. We don't need more time, resources, or support. We don't need more confidence or reassurance. We don't need to know more than we know. We don't need proof for our assumptions.

The consciousness we bring to uncertainty is created by our language. Consciousness is language. The very language we use to describe our life, world, problems, and possibilities is either more madness or magic. Language creates our experience.

As unlikely as it seems, all it takes to flourish in uncertainty is a shift from the language of assumptions to the language of questions.

Paths

s counterintuitive as it seems, organizing uncertainty is not about creating certainty or the illusion of it.

Organizing uncertainty is about turning swarms of uncertainties into opportunity and path questions. Questions instantly focus us into constructive actions of discovery.

An opportunity is a set of circumstances that makes it possible to do something. These are given and created circumstances.

In any experience of uncertainty, an opportunity question is about something we want to know how to do. Opportunity questions are *how can we* questions.

Every time we have organized uncertainty into something meaningful, it was because we could do something we previously did not know how to do.

Our life narrative is woven with stories of achievement and survival. We've achieved gains and survived losses. We've survived setbacks and crises, tragedies and triumphs.

Each celebration of achieving and surviving happened precisely because we became able to do something we previously didn't know how to do. New abilities grew, with or without definitive goals or plans.

In any new challenge, change, passion, and project, each experience of uncertainty is a chance to realize something we want to know how to do.

In moments of self-doubt, we want to know how to be decisive. In moments of tension with others we want to know how to be our best self. In moments of overwhelm, we want to know how to feel focused.

In moments of stress, we want to know how to make the difficult easy. In moments of feeling lost, we want to know how to find our way to what matters most to us. In moments of chaos, we want to know how to create order.

We turn everything we want to know how to do into opportunity questions. Each new success achieved is a new opportunity question realized. A path method begins with forming opportunity questions. Paths answer these questions.

Questions work because, unlike assumptions, they're entirely based on reality.

Organizing uncertainty begins the moment we choose our opportunity questions. Just choosing them releases us from the undertow of uncertainty. We feel an immediate shift toward greater clarity.

We don't need to have all the right answers to form good questions. We don't have to first or ever defend and prove our assumptions right.

When we're clear on our questions, uncertainty is a fertile space of possibility. Life becomes an endless adventure of discovery.

As soon as uncertainty becomes a fertile space of discovery, it becomes perfectly alright to experience uncertainty. Uncertainty no longer feels like clear evidence of personal failure, deficiency, or ineptitude. It feels like an infinite possibility space, an unplanned gift.

How do we form our opportunity questions?

We begin by choosing a path opportunity of uncertainty to work with. This can be any kind of challenge, change, passion, or project.

We then identify our path inspirations for this opportunity. These are the benefits of working on our chosen uncertainty. A benefit is any good that might come from working on any uncertainty opportunity.

Let's say we have an opportunity focused on being active. We identify a benefit of this opportunity, which could be to have more energy when we need it.

Our creating more energy benefit has benefits. One could be getting more done early in the morning before the business and buzz of the day.

We can peel off as many layers of benefits as we want because all benefits have benefits. These are our path inspirations.

Identifying benefits and benefits of benefits deepens our understanding of our chosen path opportunity. It extends our perspective on how our work in the present can have meaning far beyond the present, into the future. It makes it easier to shape paths that organize the uncertainty of our opportunity.

This sets up forming our opportunity questions that will shape our paths.

How does this work?

Considering our chosen opportunity and opportunity inspirations, we decide what we want to know how to do as a result of working on this opportunity. We form these into opportunity questions.

The vocabulary of opportunity questions is rich and varied. There are at least a dozen lenses to reveal them.

What are we passionate about? What would we love to see possible at any point in the future? What matters to us? What would give our life new forms of meaning, joy, or delight?

What do we value and cherish? What do we think our purpose in life is? What could be a good or great use of our talents? What would we love to learn, explore, or discover?

What problems do we want to solve for? What problems do we want to have? What's the impossible we would love to see possible? What would we most want for our future self, others, and our world?

Each of these represents something we want to know how to to. We use these to create our initial, draft opportunity questions.

Draft opportunity questions don't need to feel finished and definitive. They are our first sense of opportunity questions. They will grow and evolve in the process.

How do we then transition from our draft opportunity questions to our working opportunity questions?

We start a list of our knowns: what we know relative to our draft opportunity questions.

What we know includes what's already clear, what is true, what is fact, and what we have evidence for, as well as the resources, time, talents, and connections we have available.

Then we make a list of our unknowns: what we don't yet know.

What we don't know includes anything we think we need to discover, learn, research, confirm, or decide as well as anything that is an assumption, expectation, or speculation. Assumptions include what we think we need.

Our actionable unknowns become our path
questions.

Based on our opportunity inspirations, knowns
and unknowns, we craft our working
opportunity questions. These will shape our
paths. We can have one or many.

*How do our opportunity questions have the power to
organize uncertainty?*

We answer our opportunity questions through
action on our path questions.

Paths are emergent sequences of actionable
questions that answer our opportunity
questions. Path questions are in the forms of:
*who, what, when, where, why, how, which, what if,
could we, should we, what would it look like if,* and
what would it take to.

We form as many questions for our paths as we
can from any actionable unknowns. For each
path question, we name at least one path action
that could answer it.

Path actions include verbs like: exploring, looking into, confirming, researching, sketching, visualizing, experimenting, deciding, and creating the conditions for something.

If we find we have questions that lack actions, we focus instead on any that are actionable. One way to add more path questions is considering if there are any that should precede or follow ones we already have.

Let's say we have the opportunity question: *How can we complete each day feeling like we made good use of our time?* We can create paths of questions to make progress on this opportunity question.

Several path questions are possible. When are we making good use of unexpected shifts and changes in our calendars? What could we try to make better use of these shifts and changes? What can tell us we're making good use of our time? What could progress look like?

Everything we do to answer our path questions helps us answer our opportunity questions.

Each path question answered reveals new path questions.

The power of path questions is how they lead to actions rather than assumptions, progress rather than perfection.

In the uncertainty of career transition, let's say we have an opportunity question: *How can we find work that works with our life as it is and that we would find meaningful to do?*

A variety of path questions can emerge from this opportunity question. Here are just a few of many possible.

What organizations we would like to work for have jobs related to our interests? We can answer this by the exploring around and interviewing people.

Can we apply for jobs where we can learn skills that make us more prepared for a variety of future jobs? We can answer this by looking into jobs that could provide us exposure to new kinds of learning.

What kinds of work might be attractive to us? We can answer these by visualizing ourselves in a variety of different work environments, seeing how each feels, and noticing patterns.

How can we best represent ourselves at this point? We can answer this by experimenting with ideas for a website featuring our experience, career interests, and talents.

Each answer from these path questions will lead to new questions and possibilities of progress.

We're not trying to prove any assumptions right. We are simply answering our opportunity questions, one path question at a time.

We make a career transition that makes sense and works because we're working the whole time from the reality of questions rather than assumptions.

Organizing uncertainty through opportunity and path questions works because it keeps us entirely realistic and mindful.

In contrast to plans where we need to detail the complete schedule of actions to reach our goal, we don't need a ton of path questions to work from because work on each question reveals the next questions for our path of progress.

It sounds like opportunity and path questions are fluid, perhaps even unpredictable.

Imagine rock climbing. We scan the reality of the rocks before us, taking stock of what we know and don't know.

We get clear on the direction of our opportunity and make progress, one step at a time.

Our sense of opportunity and next steps shifts with each step taken. On our best climbs, each next step is discovered, not planned. Future steps remain unpredictable and are revealed only with each next step.

Our momentum is entirely based on how we move forward from curiosity and discovery rather than assumptions. Our opportunity questions are our directions; our path questions are our steps.

Many times in uncertainty, the questions tend to be stress-inducing and not particularly productive. How do we form the right questions?

The difference between fertile and futile path questions is the extent to which we understand our opportunity question knowns and unknowns.

If we don't understand these, we waste time in stressful, unproductive, futile path questions. When we understand them, we engage in meaningful, productive path questions.

With an opportunity question of how to develop a healthy variety of cooking, we know we have access to unlimited recipes and videos. We know our areas of confidence and challenge. We know people who cook well, and are healthier than most.

These are our knowns. They are reality, not assumptions.

In any form of uncertainty, what's known is dynamic. It shifts and changes as reality shifts and changes, and as we move forward with questions.

On our ever-churning list of unknowns, we are not sure what new recipes we would find attractive. We're not sure if we will have time to try new recipes. We're not sure what kinds of foods might be healthier for us than others.

We're not sure who we know who cooks well and might be willing to cook with us. We're not sure if we have an adequately stocked and equipped kitchen. All of these are unknowns.

Each of these instances of unclarity are ripe opportunities for the assumptions of our opinions, guesses, and speculations for which we don't have facts. Each also can be turned into a possible question for our path.

The lure and gravitas of our assumptions can make them feel like facts. Because something feels true doesn't mean it necessarily is. Our brain has the biochemical ability to make something feel entirely true even when it entirely isn't.

As we identify our unknowns, we can divide these into actionable and non-actionable. Non-actionable unknowns get translated into questions we put further down our paths. We focus all our energies on our actionable questions, those we can take action on.

Common non-actionable questions are explanations of why things are as they are, speculations of what will happen, interpretations of what something means, and worries of what could be.

In any kind of uncertainty, we are capable of coming up with all kinds of fascinating and frustrating questions that seem urgent or important, and likely non-actionable.

They are the kinds of questions we can most easily and unproductively obsess over. Question obsessions are signs of unknowables.

In our cooking opportunity, what's non-actionable now is how much we will eventually achieve, how much unplanned time we will have for cooking, and what impacts cooking will have on our energy and life.

Some of what's unknown is also actionable. What we don't know but could know includes things we could explore, visualize, experiment with, and create the conditions for.

What are some of the more highly reviewed and recent cookbooks and blogs we can explore? What new forms of cooking seem important now? What would it look like to have an easy time preparing new things?

What would it be like to experiment with a new recipe with ingredients we're familiar with? When would we have the most time to put together one healthy meal? Can we share what we learn with friends and family?

*Do paths work with any kind of opportunity
questions?*

In each experience of uncertainty, there are
things we know, things we don't know, things
we can't know, and things we can know through
action.

We want to know how to write a book, start a
family, retire enjoyably, survive a diagnosis, say
last goodbyes, revive or refresh a partnership,
shift professions or trades, launch or sell a
business, make an investment, travel, take up
any kind of creative pursuit, volunteer, or
cultivate a new ecology of friends.

We can turn each into a rich opportunity
question, or several path questions.

Any areas of our life where we have goals or
plans, or where we think we should have goals
or plans, are also ripe possibility spaces for the
magic of opportunity and path questions.

How possible and useful is it to put commitment timelines on opportunity questions?

When it comes to opportunity questions and timelines, a few options are possible and useful. We can have timed, untimed, and timeless questions.

Timed questions are time specific. We want to work on specific opportunity question until an event of some kind, like moving into a new job or residence. We can dedicate some months or a year to an opportunity question.

Untimed opportunity questions are open ended. We will decide down the road if and when we might to continue work on them. In the meantime, we work on questions for as long as they have meaning for us.

Timeless questions are those we are committed to working on for the rest of our lives. They have deep lifelong significance for us. We can turn any lifelong commitment, passion, or goal into a timeless question.

So, we develop path questions from our actionable questions. How does that work?

From our actionable questions of what we *could* know, we create path questions of what we *want* to know that could make possible progress from our opportunity questions.

Take a simple opportunity question about how we can eat and cook healthier dishes: *How can we grow a productive garden in the small spaces we have available?*

To shape our path of questions from this opportunity question, we form actionable path questions.

Exploring questions give us more insight, perspective, and understanding into any of our actionable (knowable) unknowns.

How has anyone has done this, and what could we learn from them? What kinds of articles and videos are out there? We work on each question by looking into something.

What if we try one pot or container to grow something simple? We work on each question by experimenting with something, with the purpose of discovering, not proving.

What would it look and feel like to be able to cook familiar and unfamiliar recipes with what our garden produces?

We work on each question by imagining different options and noticing how each feels. We use visualizing with *should we* and *could we* questions. These are choices we consider based on feelings and intuition when we don't have data for decision making.

What would it take to have a quarter of our meal ingredients come from our garden? What would it take to cook new recipes with what we grow? We work on each question by creating the conditions for any kind of progress we want to make happen.

We shape as many path questions as we want. As we go forward, we can add to, edit, delete, and reorder them.

How do we know which questions to work on?

When we work on paths, we always work on
our most important path questions. These are
the questions we will answer before others.

As questions emerge, we list and sequence them
in a practical and responsive order. We adjust
the order of our questions to accommodate what
we discover along the path.

In sequencing our questions, we pay attention to
two things: dependencies and timing.

Some things functionally need to happen before
others can. Research questions come before
design questions, building questions come
before testing questions.

Some things best happen within certain
windows of time when conditions and resources
are optimal. We plant seeds when they are most
likely to germinate.

As we move along paths, we keep updating the
order of our path questions.

Is it important or useful to set measurable success indicators so we know if we're failing or succeeding on our paths?

Unlike goals that have ends, opportunities are endless. Opportunity questions focus on *the best possible* version of whatever we want to know how to do.

If we have an opportunity question of how we can launch and grow a new business, our path questions focus on how we can launch and grow the best possible version of this business.

Even though the nature of this best possible version is unpredictable, we will discover and create what's possible, one path question at a time. We can set any success metrics we want, but none of them make anything predictable. Opportunity questions and paths can reach out weeks or lifetimes.

We never run out of opportunity questions because there is always some kind of uncertainty. We never run out of path questions because there are always things that are likely knowable.

We are continuously inspired, energized, and organized by our curiosity. We can't get stuck or distracted because we're always working on our most important path questions with the time we have.

As opportunity questions make our life wonderfully interesting, the possibilities of an interesting life has no limits.

What about deadlines? They tend to play a critical role in goals and plans.

The illusion of deadlines is that they are supposed to make things happen. That said, everyone who misses deadlines has deadlines. As good as they look good on paper, deadlines are assumptions, and as such are not necessarily realistic.

In the worst case, deadlines tell us how long we have to procrastinate. Putting anything off creates energy-sapping resistance that makes action less likely and putting off more likely. This creates drag on momentum.

Deadlines layer onto uncertainty more uncertainty about when we will have the time to take action. If we're over-scheduled or dependent on others with time management challenges, we suffer from the stress of doubts.

A less stressful and more realistic approach is to work from momentum. Getting things done with optimum velocity is about momentum.

For momentum, we choose how much time we will give to any path on a daily, weekly, or monthly rhythm. Even small amounts of time on a regular tempo has the ability to make progress happen that deadlines do not.

Where deadlines sap energy, momentum creates energy.

In our cooking opportunity questions, we can choose to start with 10 minutes a day on our new recipes path questions. We can accelerate or decelerate this rhythm whenever we want. This energizes our path momentum.

The key to optimum momentum is working on the right questions at the right time. This is as important as the amount of time we give to working on path questions. Working on the wrong questions or the right questions at the wrong time prevents optimal momentum.

How do schedules factor into paths?

We can choose specific dates and times to begin or complete work on any path questions.

We can update and adjust them as reality changes. Doing so makes it possible to choose the optimum momentum of work on our paths of questions.

We naturally frame optimal timing considerations as questions of *can we*. Can we get our garden planted by the first new moon of the season? We do whatever we can to find out if we can. Instead of schedule assumptions, we work from schedule questions.

Schedule questions shape momentum. They make it easier to establish and adjust path momentum.

On paths, schedules are not the assumptions of predictions. We don't assume to know what we can or can't do, or how long anything will or won't take. We simply give momentum to our most important path questions.

When anything will actually happen or get done is unknowable. We turn schedules into *can we* questions, and adjust them as new knowns and knowables come into view. Responsive schedules make optimal momentum possible.

When we create schedule questions for answering path questions, we are simply creating optimal conditions for momentum.

If path velocity is a function of how much time we give to a path, how do we find time to sustain or accelerate the velocity of a path?

There are three kinds of time to consider on paths: found time, carved time, and reclaimed time.

Found time is a space of moments, minutes, and sometimes hours between things. These are spaces of waiting for something or someone, or something canceled or rescheduled.

Carved time is time we take from something else. We can carve some margin of time off some regular activities without reducing the quality of them. The volume of time we give anything is not always equal to the value we get back. If we carve off 10 minutes off a half-dozen things a day, we have a carved hour of time to invest in accelerating momentum on any path.

Reclaimed time is time we take back from something that no longer yields value to ourselves or others. It's time that once had value but is no longer worth the opportunity cost. It is time better spent otherwise.

For people who are interested in writing a book every two years, a momentum of two pages a week, using one carved or found hour, would yield a book every other year. Momentum doesn't require large chunks of time.

How does it work when there are no end points for our directions, the way there are with goals and plans? Don't we need end points to experience a sense of reward at the conclusion of a plan?

Opportunity questions are intrinsically rewarding. Just working from them releases the same biochemicals that get released in successful goal completion.

Opportunity questions are directions, not destinations. They have no intrinsic end points because they can have an endless number of branches.

Any opportunity question can lead to other, new branches of opportunity questions.

Aren't there some kinds of uncertainty that are too chaotic to organize?

It can feel this way. Life can give us forms of uncertainty that provoke more emotion than they evoke clarity. We can be overwhelmed. All we seem to have are questions that have no easy or particularly helpful or reassuring answers.

Even in these moments of feeling lost, we can choose opportunity questions. There are always things we want to know how to do. There are always knowables that can become paths of questions that get us moving in the direction of our opportunity questions.

The more we organize uncertainty through paths, the more confidence we have in our ability to do so.

As with any art, proficiency and fluency follow practice. The more we practice, the more productive and satisfying our experience. The easier it is to organize uncertainty of any shapes and sizes. Uncertainty becomes a rich source of possibility and meaning.

Through paths, we can organize any kind of uncertainty we encounter and create in our life and our world. No assumptive or constrictive goals or plans are necessary.

It sounds simple. Is that all there is to it, just knowing our opportunity questions and moving forward along our paths?

That's all there is to it. Compared to the gravitas of goals and plans, it shouldn't work, but it does.

Why couldn't the mindfulness of opportunity and path questions have more power to organize uncertainty than the unrealistic and mindless assumptions of goals and plans?

Reality is, we can approach whatever is important or imperative to us from the constraints of goals and plans, or from the expansiveness of our questions.

All it takes is learning a new vocabulary. Learning the language of paths is fairly easy because our brains are already hardwired for mindful curiosity.

How is a path method related to mindfulness?

One of the more compelling and researched definitions of mindfulness is noticing what's new.

That's what happens on paths. We are continuously noticing the next versions of what's obvious, unknown, likely unknowable, and actionable as they emerge.

Mindfulness releases biochemicals that create our experience of curiosity and reward. It infuses the immediacy of paths with as much meaning as any distant destination. *How* becomes as satisfying as *where*.

All path mindfulness requires is curiosity and uncertainty, both of which are constantly available.

Mindfulness is often talked about as a natural antidote to stress. How are uncertainty, stress and paths related?

Every form of unwelcome stress is a form of trying to resist uncertainty. It's the anxiousness of trying to manufacture as much certainty as we think need.

It is accurate and useful to think about unwelcome stress as an indicator we're not yet organizing uncertainty. It is inaccurate and useless to assume this stress is being caused by people, events, conditions, or some form of our own failure.

As long we maintain this assumption, we prevent learning about the possibility and power of paths. We just keep going down the rabbit hole of blame. The further down the hole we go, the less visibility we have on new options, and the more we amplify the uncertainty.

The easiest transition from distress is through a path mindset.

We can bring a path mindset to anything. It applies to all of life, including and beyond organizing the usual and unusual uncertainty.

We waste less time and manufacture less unnecessary stress when we no longer struggle to answer questions that cannot be answered because we focus instead on what's knowable.

Based on our habits of language, our brains are hardwired to create stress or curiosity. The more we live from paths of opportunity questions, the less distress we experience.

Is it possible to have too many opportunity questions?

How many opportunity questions we have at any point in time depends on our cultivated capacity for curiosity. The more curious we are, the more opportunity questions we can have. We can certainly have more opportunity questions than available time or resources.

We can accommodate more opportunity questions if we size them differently. Larger opportunity questions are those we give time to more often. Smaller questions are those we give time to less often.

We can have small questions we give an hour or two monthly. We can have medium questions we give an hour or two weekly. We can have large questions we give an hour or two daily.

We can have a backlog of inactive opportunity questions we draw from and activate in some future timeframe.

When it's possible and sensible, we can resize any active question. We can give more time to a small or medium question. We can give less time to a medium or large question.

What about the problems that just seem impossible? What do we do with these?

Impossible is an assumption, an opinion and speculation. In our work on paths, we turn the uncertainty of impossible into new questions. We don't postpone action we assumptively declare as impossible.

Every innovation and breakthrough in any domain was once assumed impossible by experts, leaders, funders, and investors.

Fortunately, curious adventurers crafted opportunity and path questions and later arrived at the first or next generation of impossible.

All that mattered were the knowables that faithfully organized the swarm of unknowns. While others lived in hope or despair, they remained relentless in forming and following paths in the direction of their largest opportunity questions.

It's perfectly reasonable to work from unreasonable opportunity questions, and their promise of abundant serendipity.

We can join the countless numbers of people who have shaped incredibly rich and meaningful lives inspired by impossibilities they might or might not have ever realized.

So this path method is interesting and useful. Is there a simple way to remember the process?

Yes. It's four things.

1. We choose an opportunity to work on.
2. We create our opportunity questions.
3. We shape our path.
4. We work and update our path.

This method applies to any scale and scope of personal and collective uncertainty. It's simple, adaptable, and realistic. The shift in language turns uncertainty into magic.
The key is to start playing with the method.

One way to begin is by mapping out all the ways we experience uncertainty in our life today. This includes any aspects of life including any kind of work, obligations and interests.

We can choose one or two kinds of uncertainty to begin with and try crafting some possible opportunity questions of what we would like to be able to do in these areas of uncertainty.

We choose one or two to start with, mapping out the two context dimensions.

As we work with this, if it's unclear whether something is known or not, it's probably not and goes on the *unknowns* list. If it's unclear if something is likely unknowable or actionable, it's actionable if we can take any kind of action on it.

Keep lists, notes and all related resources in a single place like a paper or virtual notebook, or list and mindmapping apps.

Experiment with different ways to keep everything visible, accessible, and organized. Go with what works best after testing some options and versions.

If we want to put schedules to our paths, we do so, updating them as necessary. Expect schedules will shift as our new knowns, new questions, and new realities shift.

Try out different kinds of momentum tempos for any paths we're working on. See what works and adjust accordingly.

The attitude here is one of playing with possibilities, learning from experience, and adapting as we go. Any path questions will lead to better path questions.

In little time, our paths inspire and energize our life. Questions are the leverage points for us to work with reality. When we work with reality, reality works for us. We unleash the power of organizing uncertainty in any kind of challenge, change, passion, or project.

A path method

The simple power of paths in any kind of uncertainty is that they make known exactly what we need to do at any point in time.

We don't have to guess what we could or need to do. Our path questions tell us. All we need is to know our path questions, work on them in order, and revise our paths as new questions emerge.

When we have questions that call for exploring something, we have conversations, get online, take a course, or attend an event or talk.

When we have path questions that call for visualizing something, we picture in our mind's eye different versions and scenarios of how something could unfold or turn out. We see how each and each revision feels.

When we have questions that call for trying something new, we do small, timed, and critiqued experiments.

When we have questions that call for creating something, we do whatever we can to create the conditions for this. We work from a perspective of progress.

Given there are many questions we could use to start a path, is there one question we could begin any path with?

There is. It's the *what could it look like if* question.

This is the root of what we want to know how to do. What would it look like if we made good use of our time and talents this month?

This simple, powerful question mobilizes us to do whatever we can to answer it. It inspires new questions and options and engages path momentum.

It is a question that leads to all kinds of productive path questions and actions. It creates the conditions for progress in the direction of what matters to us in any context of uncertainty.

When we have no idea where to begin, we begin here. Imagination is the mother of curiosity, birthing and nurturing the generativity of our opportunity questions.

What if we think we might be missing some useful or important path questions? How do we grow more confidence in any path we're on.

It helps to get clear on our doubts and concerns. When we translate each into new questions, we raise our sense of confidence in our path.

Creating and refreshing our list of reasonable assumptions, expectations, hunches, and predictions are all grist for the question mill.

When we translate the unknown into the actionables and these into new path questions, we feel more confident on our path.

Sharing details of our path with others, especially if they've traveled similar paths, is yet another way to discover questions we haven't yet considered.

How do we make sense of data from research we do from exploring questions?

When we explore any actionable questions, and we discover new kinds of results labeled "data," path wisdom is sustaining a spirit of mindful curiosity rather than mindless belief or skepticism.

Any kind of data can raise new path questions if we approach it with a curious mind. There are simple questions that make this possible.

Are there any exceptions here? Is anyone presenting contrasting data? Could the data be gathered or interpreted in different ways? Is the data based on any assumptions, strongly held beliefs, agendas, or ideologies? Is there support for contrasting views?

The half-life of much technical and specialized information today is measured in months rather than years. This is likely to accelerate with the maturity of machine learning and artificial intelligence.

These kinds of questions minimize the risks of unconscious and conscious biases seeking proof for what we earnestly believe instead of seeking discovery from our latest path of actionable questions.

How does visualization work?

Some of our questions call for consideration of different approaches to opportunity questions we can think through because we can't do an experiment or take action otherwise.

This means visualizing different options and variations both in what we would like to see and how we could bring that about. Some questions, especially those for which we can't get more data now, are best answered with feelings and intuition.

We visualize to work out different ways to solve problems, test alternatives, play out scenarios, and build ideas. The more details, the better.

We're not trying to predict anything. Visualization is simply a lens through which to more clearly discover and test new options in the present. We're exploring how different approaches, variations, and details feel.

The power of visualizing is in listening to the feelings and intuition emerging in the process. They help clarify our leanings and learnings from what we visualize.

Visualization draws from experience, curiosity, and intuition. It can lead to exploring and experimenting questions. It reveals new, previously hidden possibilities and questions.

We don't often think of doing experiments as ways of answering questions. How do experiments work?

Small, low-cost, low-risk experiments are always more possible in uncertainty than we might think.

We make creativity most possible when we try something new as an experiment rather than something that feels more permanent.

We try out new ways of having conversations, organizing everyday work, and supporting those we care most about. We try out new ways of getting heard, making progress up mountains, staying up to date, and using our time wisely.

We try something not to prove we can, to prove our assumptions are correct, or to prove anything. The freedom to learn from whatever we experience allows us to be optimally creative, discerning, and adaptive.

When we explore our questions along any path, there are often questions that can only be addressed through small experiments.

We try something out, for a brief period of time, to gain clarity on the possibilities. Each iteration generates the next cue of questions that can lead us back to exploring or creating something new.

A micro-experiment is the smallest scale possible. The economy of micro-experiments is that they require what we have available to test one or more options.

If we want to experiment with journaling, two minutes of journaling a day could be a micro-experiment.

Feedback and learning comes in the form of our direct, unfiltered experience and the perceptions and insights of others.

The only kind of failure possible is failing to learn from our experience, which is a call for editing the design of our experiment, or deleting it and starting over using what we have learned so far.

The value of experiments is measured by the new questions and insights gained, not how well our experience satisfied our assumptive expectations.

Experimenting as a way of answering questions
seems risky when we have so many unknowns.

We get to questions on paths where it just makes
sense to try something new.

The value of experimenting is that it moves us
into action at a point where more obsession,
discussion, debate, and speculation aren't going
to get us to more or better questions or answers.

There are two kinds of experiments: fixed and
flexible. A fixed experiment cannot be redone, or
cannot be redone without unacceptable costs. A
flexible experiment can be redone.

Before we embark on any scale experiment, it's
wise to make sure we have no more unanswered
actionable questions. If we do, we answer those
first.

The other wisdom, especially in potentially
high-impact and high-cost experiments, is to
check in with trusted guides, especially people
who have successfully navigated and organized
this or similar kinds of uncertainty before.

We can get perspective from someone we trust to ask questions we overlook. We want to know if they see any unknowns we miss.

The same goes for checking in with anyone else related to this situation who might have different perspectives and directions. This is especially true for anyone who has history on current contexts and who can or will be impacted by the experiment at hand.

This simple step can dramatically help prevent and reduce risks of failure, and optimize our chance to realize our questions along the way.

What is the distinction between experimenting with and deciding?

Deciding can connote devising a final solution to a problem. Experimenting can be more about trying different options for the purpose of learning and progress.

The intention in experimenting is making things better, which is distinct from making problems go away.

It's wise to sometimes do an experiment instead of making a decision, particularly when the decision implies any number of assumptions and doubts that experiments can shed light on.

When and how is creating something a good way to answer questions on a path?

We answer some path questions by creating the conditions required.

When we want to know how to get some quality refresh time on weekends, we work on the path question of what would it take to feel refreshed on weekends. *What would it take to* is a root form of creating questions.

After some exploring or creating with different refresh options, we find out what it takes by actually taking time to start new refresh habits.

We begin with small naps, quick workouts, pure luxury reading or listening, taking walks in nature, talking with good friends we don't often get to see. We know what something takes when it's actually done.

Each action reveals what it takes to refresh on weekends. We only discover what something takes when we do what something takes.

No matter how many assumptions we might have, we only know all the conditions for making something possible the moment we actually manifest it in reality with meaningful actions.

When we create the conditions for something we want to realize, we're doing so in an attitude of curiosity rather than trying to prove any assumptions, the way we would with goals and plans.

What if we get bogged down and stall on a path? What if we get stuck, disoriented, or just unhappy with how it's going?

There is a handful of meta-questions that can help.

Are we still genuinely committed to our opportunity questions for this path ? Would it make sense to create a new version of this question that would be more compelling, inspiring, or energizing?

Would it help to increase the momentum of our efforts on this path? How could a more lively pace energize our efforts?

Are we trying to spend time on non-actionable questions instead of investing all of our time in actionable questions?

Would a different approach to answering questions help: using exploring instead of experimenting, visualizing instead of exploring, experimenting instead of creating?

One of the classic ways of getting stuck is by obsessing over getting things *perfect*. The antidote is doing what is simply *better*.

*How do we stay motivated along a path, especially
given the natural potential for energy dips, shiny
object distractions, frustrating obstacles, and
corrosive self-doubt?*

Paths don't require heroic efforts at motivation
the way goals and plans do. Where goals and
plans immediately and continuously provoke a
sense of disabling self-doubt, opportunity
questions provoke energizing curiosity.

Also, on paths, the small steps of progress
advance us along, so we are continuously
energized by a sense of being productive.

Momentum creates energy rather than depletes
it. Momentum fuels motivation. We feel like we
have energy available for the most important
questions on our path. There is no greater nor
more sustainable motivator than curiosity.

*Success and failure seem clear with goals and plans.
When we stay on plan and achieve goals, we're*

succeeding. When we don't, we're failing. In this
world of paths, what constitutes success and failure?

In a world of paths, we talk more about
discovery than success. This perspective is based
on the reality that although it is not always
possible to continuously succeed in a future
outcome, it is possible to continuously discover
from present questions.

As soon as we define success, we create the
conditions for failure. Every time we cannot
successfully follow plans, we fail. Every time we
do not achieve goals, we fail. Changing goals
and plans also imply failure to follow and
achieve them in their original forms.

This is why few of us are thrilled when we set or
are assigned goals, or make or get assigned to
plans. We spend an unacceptable amount of our
time in failure mode.

In a path world, we talk about discovery and
progress. Discovering means working from our
opportunity and path questions.

We can do some discovering whenever we want. Life doesn't have to be abundant with certainty and predictability. Uncertainty is a prime condition for discovery.

We don't have to engineer control over most of our world and ourselves. We don't have to make heroic or egoic sacrifices for some distant, if untenable, success. We don't have to measure our happiness and worth in units of achievement. Progress and discovery is our joy.

Discovering is always possible as long as we have uncertainty and know how to translate it into the language of questions.

Why could we get stuck on a path, even though we're clear on and committed to our opportunity questions?

There are two common reasons. We get stuck when we work on good questions at the wrong time. We get stuck when we work on wrong questions for any time.

Good questions at the wrong time are usually questions focused on non-actionable questions. These are speculative questions that can't be accurately answered given what we don't know. If they can be answered, it will be later down a path.

Working on these squanders valuable time from actionable questions we can answer through some form of exploring or creating.

Questions that are not useful make us feel counterproductively powerless, anxious, depressed, blaming, or retaliative. They evoke obsessive thinking and talking, various forms of emotional numbing, and certainly no productive or constructive action.

Because a question feels compelling or urgent and that comes up in our personal consciousness or shared conversations doesn't in any way indicate it has the power to move us forward on any path. That people with volume or power think a question is important doesn't necessarily mean it is.

All kinds of freedom occur when we understand shifting out of stuckness simply takes shifting from the language of shame and blame to the language of opportunity and path questions.

It's that simple and possible. It doesn't require trauma or drama. It doesn't require therapeutic labeling or changes in our personalities or the right mix of slippery and spiraling incentives. It doesn't require lowering our standards or downsizing or outsourcing our expectations.

We can begin where we are. We can begin with what we have. We are enough and have enough. It's just a matter of discovering and practicing a new language.

Is it best to have one path for each of our opportunity questions?

One path can work. It's also possible that multiple paths could be more interesting, even more productive, because there can be multiple right ways to move in the direction of any opportunity question.

We can start two new businesses, gardens, classes, house projects, weekend routines. Where planning can often be a single, linear succession of actions toward a single goal, path shaping can involve multiple paths from single opportunity questions.

In more situations than what might seem obvious, there can be two or more "right ways" to move in the direction of any opportunity question. Because one path option emerges first, or has more historical precedents, it does not mean it is the only or best path possible.

The advantage is that working on multiple paths concurrently makes work on each richer. It can lead to one path becoming a new branch to graft onto another, more mature path. It can lead to the mergers of paths into more robust paths.

Accomplished artists often concurrently work on multiple pieces, projects, and bodies of work. What they find is that each one is a path that becomes a lens revealing new opportunities for other paths.

When they move from one to another, the work from one reveals new possibilities and questions in another. Each path is richer for the other lenses at work and at play.

With artistic opportunity questions in painting, writing, or home brewing, we can work along multiple concurrent paths of going to local classes, learning online, time bartering with a tutor, and experimenting on our own.

In starting a new business or side hustle, we can move along two or more ways to pursue this. Because we're moving along through questions and not assumptions, we are always on solid ground.

In some kinds of uncertainty, we can have and work from contradictory directions.

We can want to know how to make the best of a current situation *and* know how to pivot to a different scenario. We don't necessarily have to choose between them. Working on both makes work on each richer and can lead to opportunity coherence.

Reality, revealed through action, will tell us the potential value and costs of each step we take. Our new unknowns from our actions along all paths will tell exactly what to do next because they will reveal our next iteration of questions.

It will become clear if we should edit, add, graft, merge, detach, or delete any active paths. The strategy of multiple paths is an infinitely more creative and realistic approach than putting all of our progress eggs in the basket of a singular, assumption-based goal and plan.

How does timing factor into how we approach paths?

A mindful approach is to time actions in sync with optimal conditions in our world. This involves being curious about and giving attention to what's going on around us.

Being in sync gives us a unique kind of velocity because we do things when the conditions are optimal. It's based on the notion that there are better times than others to act on our questions.

When any of these are knowable, our sense of timing rewards our mindfulness.

All this simply means is that even as we start shaping a path, we keep timing foreground as we form our questions and sequence and time our actions. It's cutting with the grain, sailing with the wind, flowing with the stream.

Why is the idea of progress so important when working on paths?

Because we have no predictable end points for opportunity questions, we focus on a seamless stream of progress. Path progress is golden.

An attitude of progress is the opposite of an attitude of perfection. In a perfection perspective, we remain anxious about getting our goal and plan assumptions "right."

A focus on perfection slows down momentum, prevents new ideas, erodes optimism and self-efficacy, increases resistance to anything new, rigidifies thinking, and turns motivation into a roller coaster.

A focus on progress strengthens self-efficacy, boosts a growth mindset, and optimizes adaptability. It turns every experience into discovery.

At the point where we begin to organize uncertainty, we can create language for what progress means. We can describe the questions and actions that represent clear progress along our paths.

Progress can be described as what 1% of movement in any direction could look like.

The power of this question is the reality that 1% daily progress in 100 days leads to 100% progress. The dream of the possible and impossible begins in the humble origins of uncertainty navigated in the smallest of steps.

Our definition of progress will shift as we move along our paths. Progress from point B to point C will look different than progress from point A to point B. If we overestimate what progress means, we simply scale back to what is doable.

Progress creates the adjacent possible. These are options that only become possible and visible after other kinds of progress have been achieved. Cells phones became the adjacent possible only after certain milestones were achieved in internet, communications, and other predecessor technologies.

The adjacent possible makes the consequences of progress unpredictable, if not exponential. Unlike the postponed, and often unreachable success of goals, progress means we are in continuous discovery.

How much organizing and preventing uncertainty is about being busy? Can busy be an effective antidote to uncertainty?

If it's unclear what we have in common with our neighbors on the planet, there is a reasonable probability we share a bias for being busy.

We're busy working on better lives, flourishing families, and rewarding careers. We're busy keeping up with friends and trends, and improvising the next chapters of our life.

Busy has become a badge of esteem and convenience, a reason for brag and excuse. We measure success and self-worth in units of things done.

It's possible to get addicted to busy. We resist saying no and think time management is our problem. Our calendars brim with shoulds.

The Chinese character for busy is composed of two syllables, "heart" and "death."

The prime tools of busy are goals and plans. By design, they keep us feeling we never have or are enough. They keep us busy in a chronically-behind life of deferred rewards.

What if it could be otherwise? What if we could derive as much joy in journeys as we do in arrivals? What if doing became as meaningful as done?

By design, we would need alternatives to goals and plans. We would discover that we can't goal and plan our way into making the richness of the journey at least as significant as the reach of the destination.

We would need to have a way to make the path the point. This is the radical manifesto of a path method.

Is uncertainty fatigue a thing, where uncertainty wears us down and depletes our energy and confidence? Isn't uncertainty the true root cause of any kind of burn out?

The uncertainty of change can evoke a sense of stressful and overwhelming self-doubt. Lack of a clear way forward makes us question our ability to navigate our way into what we want to see possible.

Self-doubt is why we react to uncertainty with resistance rather than resilience. Getting lost in swirls of self-doubt puts us into our self-sabotaging fear brain.

Having confidence in our ability to organize uncertainty well is self-efficacy. Self-efficacy propels us forward on paths and gives us the creativity, adaptability, and persistence to move around and beyond obstacles.

Self-efficacy is why we can turn uncertainty into the delight of realized paths.

The practice

**W**orking from path questions gets easier when we cultivate a curious mind.

It's a simple practice.

Whatever situation we find ourself in, we mindfully notice what's unknown. What's unclear, unknown, unconfirmed? What could be explored beyond what we already know? What's likely knowable?

The more we practice this, the easier it becomes to shape our opportunity and path questions.

We naturally and gradually lose interest in acting from our assumptions and the assumptions of others. We cultivate more interest in our questions.

We lose faith in the illusion of certainty produced by our even best looking and sounding goals and plans. We get more

uncertainty organized than ever. It shows up in
how we show up.

Isn't failure to achieve goals and follow plans
basically a failure in people being held accountable for
them or a failure in people holding themselves
accountable for them?

It is a bizarre notion that anyone would hold
themselves or others accountable for the
assumptions of goals and plans.

When we get clear that assumptions and reality
are two qualitatively different phenomenon, we
get clear that it makes no sense to hold someone
accountable for something that is not reality.

When we have an honest relationship with the
future, we anticipate that any number of things
can change within minutes after goals and plans
have been pronounced, declared, or approved.

Decision makers can change their minds on
priorities, resources, and expectations. People
working on goals and plans can have new and

better unplanned ideas on how to get things done than was originally expected.

Any number of conditions, resources, and constraints can change.

Just the fact that everyone is working from assumptions rather than questions means questions accumulate and snowball into avalanches.

The threat of "holding" ourselves or others "accountable" for the illusion of predictability in goals and plans is unrealistic when changes are inevitable.

We don't have to be held accountable for our opportunity questions. Just having them is intrinsically meaningful. They keep us naturally inspired and engaged. We don't need overt or covert threats or bribes to move forward.

What do we do with the range of emotions that emerge and dominate us while we're organizing uncertainty and moving along paths?

We experience a variety of emotional shifts in the course of uncertainty. Emotions range from acute to subtle, momentary to enduring.

We usually tag each emotion as desirable, acceptable, unacceptable, or irrelevant. Tags amplify and intensify the tonal vibe of emotions.

The most useful tag for any emotion is the tag of reminder.

Tagging any emotion as a reminder works because every emotion in human experience can remind us of what we care about, what we consider essential and preferred. In this way, each emergent emotion can be a lens revealing our most significant questions.

I get how a path method works with less traumatic forms of uncertainty like becoming healthier. How does it work with more emotionally demanding forms of uncertainty like major losses of any kind?

We lose loved ones, jobs, our health, things we worked hard for. These are dramatic forms of uncertainty because the grief and overwhelm can be disorienting.

We begin a path method as usual with identifying all the things we want to know how to do. One opportunity question is: *What would be best use of the time we now have, created by our loss?*

For each opportunity question, we do whatever we can to understand the context of what's obvious, unknown, likely unknowable, and likely knowable.

There can be a temptation to try understanding, changing, or expressing negative feelings related to our loss. This only amplifies and sustains them.

Feelings shift and diminish in our consciousness the more we focus on crafting our opportunity questions, mapping their contexts, and working along our paths of questions.

We take our time with this because doing this as thoroughly as possible will allow us to have productive questions for our path in the direction of our opportunity questions.

The possibilities are many. Let's say we have the path question: *How can we can get out to connect with new people?*

We can explore options online and ask around; we can visualize different kinds of people and conversations we might like to connect with; we can experiment with reaching out through text; and we can realize the conditions for new connections by inviting others to something we would both enjoy.

We choose the daily and weekly momentum of working on our questions that works for us. Each action reveals our next most important opportunity and path questions.

We notice and work on any and all new emerging opportunity and path questions. We organize the uncertainty. We come through better than ever.

Paths seem counterintuitive. It's hard to imagine making things happen without relying on the assumptions of guesses, opinions, and speculations.

An interesting exercise is to take the terminal point of any goal and list all the assumptions implied it.

What does this goal assume is true today and will be true all the way to its predicted completion? We can do the same with any plans projected forward. What do they assume is true today and will be true going forward?

The lists of assumptions are generally not short. They represent all the ways we can get distracted, detoured, and derailed in the process. We can look back at any failed goals or plans and see assumptions at the root of our struggles and demise.

Even if we're in the thick of goals and plans, we can take this assumptions list and simply turn any we can into the gold of new questions on our paths. All that matters is our questions.

What happens in our brain when we don't know how to organize everyday uncertainty?

When we do not have a viable way to navigate uncertainty, we live in a space of fear.

Fear shuts down the parts of our brain involved in mindful curiosity and adaptive creativity. In our fear brain, we look for ways to avoid and resist uncertainty. We lose access to options and resources.

We retreat into the appearance of certainty in the assumptions of goals and plans.

In our fear brain, our priority is being right over being curious. We become situationally learning disabled in a fixed mindset.

A growth mindset allows for the depth and breadth of what we don't know. The unknowns and curiosity become expansive gifts and spaces of opening and discovery.

Is there a tendency for us to do more of the same when we get into our fear brain?

That's exactly what happens. When our doubts create more uncertainty, we become self-protective and resist taking risks, which means doing anything different or new.

We play it safe doing more of the same. We hope it works. This has no power to organize uncertainty into a future different from the past. Repeating the past repeats the past.

This is why goals and plans can fail. We're doing what we know, leaving the potential questions of uncertainty unrevealed and unengaged. A different future becomes possible when we get out of our fear brain by leveraging the power of what we don't know.

Can organizations of any kind and scale transition to a path method?

It depends on the extent to which people still believe goals and plans have the power to organize uncertainty or control people.

Whether these beliefs are strong or weak, the practice of goals and plans will persist in the absence of credible and compelling alternatives.

The transition takes experiential learning by doing.

It's easy learning that can happen parallel to efforts in goals and plans. It can begin in organizing any kinds of projects and work flows, decisions and problem solving, design and redesign.

The shift allows us to discover how engaging and shared questions make us smarter together. It creates space for all voices and views to make us better together.

Luck seems to be a reality in any kind of personal and collective endeavor. How would we factor luck into a path method?

Working from paths of questions creates the conditions for our own luck. Luck is the serendipity of things unplanned. Serendipity is real. We can create the conditions for it. When we take an empty seat in a public space, we create the conditions for serendipity.

When we organize uncertainty through endless discovery, we make it more possible for us to stumble on unpredictable perspectives and possibilities. New questions have this ability.

New perspectives and possibilities are by definition unpredictable. They are obscured by our attempts to organize uncertainty through the assumptions of what we already think we know.

Only when we go into the space of questions do we have access to the unpredictable. Questions unleash the power of the unpredictable.

Some of our most favorite and important people in our life showed up unplanned. Some of our best opportunities emerged unplanned. Some of our most useful ideas and breakthroughs emerged unplanned.

Much of what we feel grateful for every day occurs outside the scope of our best laid plans and goals. We don't goal and plan into existence the countless people who make possible what we are able to do every day.

A path question of *how can we create our own luck* can evoke all kinds of productive luck-friendly questions and actions. As each assumption makes us unluckier, each question makes us luckier.

How do we remain realistic when it comes to deciding what we're capable of doing on any given path ?

It's interesting to consider things in our life to date that we thought about doing, and didn't.

In how many cases did we postpone or resist pursuing something because we simply weren't sure how to organize the uncertainty? Why is it that we overestimate what we can achieve in the short term and underestimate what we can in the long term?

How many times did we not take first steps because we didn't feel confident we would succeed in some kind of goal?

What's interesting is how often our prediction of potential success is an invalid assumption.

Reality is, we cannot ever know our potential before acting on our questions. We discover it as we move forward. It is not what we think it is. It is unknowable. It can't be predicted, especially from past facts and fictions.

When we reflect on the best things in our life, and look back two or three years prior, it's clear we could have had no sense of the potential realized in these best things.

As sincere any opportunity question seems, we can't know if we can answer it. Propelled by the inspiration and momentum of relentless curiosity, we're inspired just to see if we can.

*How important, and possible, is it to be consistent
when we're moving along paths?*

Every human life is a life of contradictions. We
sometimes want things both ways. We are
attracted to opposites.

That's why when people urge us to "just decide"
on a focus, we can be attracted to multiples
rather than singular.

While we seek to simply our lives, we want the
freedom to buy and collect what suits and
soothes us. We want food that provides as much
creature comfort as nutritional virtue. We want
thriving work lives and flourishing personal
lives.

We want to go to bed late, get up early, and get
enough sleep. We want to know what's going on
in the world and not get distracted. We want our
children to enjoy a sense of freedom as long as
it's the kind we would most favor, forgive, or
approve. We did not bring them into the world
to spend the rest of their lives worrying us.

We want it both ways.

For any opportunity question we could have, it's possible to have contrasting and opposing opportunity questions. We could discover why both-and is much more useful and realistic than either-or.

A path method amply supports us organizing the uncertainty of contradictions.

As always, our questions along the way will guide us to see exactly what we can and can best do. We will find and create branches from different opportunity questions that merge into new and satisfying both-and integrations.

In a goals and plans world, people are accustomed to knowing what to expect, in as measurable and dependable terms as possible. How do we shape expectations in a world of paths?

This question is about managing expectations of people who want to know what we think our most dependable assumptions are.

In a path world, we don't have any such dependable assumptions about anything, including and especially what the actual outcomes will be and and when they will arrive.

Our most honest transparency is about our active and next opportunity and path questions. People have the highest confidence in us when they are clear that we are being as realistic, mindful, and responsive as possible.

All we can promise and deliver is seamless dedication to and real time transparency about our questions, schedule, and momentum.

We can promise to support their mindful attention to anything new in our process. We can promise to communicate clearly about anything they can do to add velocity, quality, and wisdom to the process and outcomes.

We can promise we will help them remain, as realistic, mindful, and responsive as possible.

If their intolerance of uncertainty causes them to require the consolation of assumptions, we can produce as many as they would like, making clear exactly how we have translated and prioritized them into new questions for our paths.

When they want to reprioritize our path questions, we can have those conversations and indicate the costs and benefits of any potential changes so we together make the wisest choices possible.

With more exposure to a path method, they discover the many profound and practical advantages of a path method over goals and plans in organizing uncertainty.

Intersecting paths

W hen we come together to organize uncertainty, we each bring our own perspectives.

This happens for us as partners and families, organizations and communities, networks and nations.

We come together with similar and different voices and views, visions and values. What we know and don't know feeds to our alignments and tensions.

We share a world of unprecedented uncertainties.

We face the complexities and implications of global financial and social interdependencies, political and climate immigration, technology breakthroughs and vulnerabilities, generational rifts and drifts.

Most jobs that will be awaiting today's youngest don't even yet exist. Medical abilities to keep people alive outpace social abilities to assure an elastic quality of life.

The most predictable dimension of being human is unpredictability.

It's time we figured out how to together organize uncertainty in the most practical, collaborative, and ethical ways possible. Our emerging world is far too complex, interdependent, and dynamic for us to be unrealistic, isolated, or unethical in how we organize uncertainty.

We become capable of organizing uncertainty when we together craft shared questions. Our personal and collective futures will depend on getting our questions right.

What about when we are not on the same page, even and especially when doing so would benefit all of us?

It happens. We're at odds with each other. Trust is unbuilt, fragile, or compromised. We don't have shared opportunities or paths.

Creating the possibility of shared opportunity questions can happen in a few ways.

We can begin talking about any kind of uncertainty we are now personally experiencing. We can talk about the contexts of each. Understanding each other's uncertainty contexts builds the trust of shared perspective, which is essential for shared questions.

We can explore how we can support each other in our opportunity questions and paths. If we find questions we do or can share, we can shape shared paths together.

This gets us on same pages. Only from same pages can we create new shared pages.

When it comes to shaping meaningful and trust-rich relationships, how important is it that we know each other's opportunity questions?

There is a simple and unique power in knowing each other's opportunity questions.

Knowing each other's daily tasks and toils, compliments and complaints does not necessarily reveal each other's opportunity questions.

We cannot support each other's questions or join in them if they aren't transparent. They cannot always be accurately interpreted, intuited, or predicted.

Also, knowing each other's questions puts us in an optimal place for deeper shared understanding and support. When we know each other's uncertainties and questions, we are in a prime position for empathy and being helpful to each other.

What about the uncertainties of people who perplex us?

We have always had, and will always have, people in our life and world who perplex us. What they do, say, want, or feel doesn't make sense to us. They test our patience and wear us down, and out. They could be genetically related to or distant from us. They are sources of uncertainty more than predictability.

Using a path method, we get clear on our opportunity questions with them. What do we want to know how to do with them?

As we choose our opportunity questions, we name the potential benefits of each, which become branch questions.

As new assumptions, interpretations, and speculations emerge along the way, we turn these into questions for our paths. Assumptions include worries, concerns, and complaints.

We sequence our opportunity questions to choose our most important, which are the ones we will work on first.

We then take our most important questions and map out their contexts of obvious, unknown, likely unknowable, and likely knowable. From our actionable questions, we form our path questions and decide for each which of the four path actions we will use to answer them.

We keep working on our next opportunity questions and include on our list any new ones that emerge. We create the possibility of showing up with our best self.

One of the more common venues for intersecting directions is at work. What are the prime possibilities for intersecting opportunities there?

Whether it's going well or it's a struggle, uncertainty is the nature of work.

There is a change in leadership or direction. Budgets and resources are stressed. We're continuously expected to get less and do more.

Our survival feels at risk. We're expanding at a challenging rate. We're failing to expand at a compelling rate. We keep getting new goals layered on top of those we have not yet realized.

We have new members who don't seem to fit. We wonder if we should be elsewhere. The culture feels stuck or strained. The work we're doing we don't want to do forever. Our impending retirement keeps us distracted from being engaged in the present.

Each is an experience of uncertainty. Each is an opportunity to create and refresh shared questions.

The transition from uncertainty to clarity begins with everyone learning a path method. This is experiential learning by doing, ideally in teams.

It doesn't matter what kind of uncertainty we apply the method. Since goals and plans are endless sources of uncertainty, we can learn and apply the method in any area of goal or with any kind of plan.

We don't have to invest in a mammoth top-down push or change management effort. It doesn't have to be mandated because it naturally makes sense. It doesn't need to be scaled, because it will naturally spread.

It doesn't need fancy measurement systems because the impact stories will be known and shared.

What about in community?

Community is a different landscape.
Communities are neighborhoods, villages, cities,
regions, and networks.

Unlike organizations, there is no one in charge
of everyone. New businesses, projects, and
initiatives come about because of the
entrepreneurship of individuals, not the
commands and controls of senior leaders or
institutional administrators.

With the exception of membership controlled
communities, anyone can join or leave
communities. People can act entirely on their
own opportunity questions or in mutual
collaboration with others on questions shared.

No one reports to anyone else who decides what
they will do, who they will associate with, what
they will learn or how they will learn it, what
work they pursue, or how they make or don't
make use of available services and resources.

What is possible in communities is that formal and informal leaders can connect people with common kinds of uncertainty and opportunity questions. This can be done in personal conversations, open meetings and meetups, and through social technologies.

They can support the development of informal and formal path method experts who can support the creation of groups and teams who share work on common opportunity and path questions. Questions connect people.

These experts can also develop ways for storytelling to spread inspiring narratives coming from these efforts.

How do opportunity and path questions factor into things like strategy, mission, vision, and values?

There are few things that can divide even the most well-intended and talented people as can messy and endless debates on mission, vision, values, and strategy.

Even when there are officially imposed definitions for each, everyone has their own definitions and priorities. The clash and unalignment of definitions make the organization of uncertainty more than necessary.

The fact that they get quickly shelved and forgotten doesn't help either.

In a path method, anything we would consider mission, vision, values, and strategy is ideal material for the formation of new opportunity and path questions.

We can shape opportunity questions for two quarters or two decades. Each next question reveals new other possible questions. We create responsive sequences of our opportunity questions so we can always work on the most important ones.

We craft and graft new branch questions, which allows for deeper as well as more inclusive and sustainable directions.

Existing and created teams, committees, and groups can take on any of the next important questions. They form paths and momentum.

This saves valuable time from unproductive and unnecessary discussions and debates. It accelerates the organization of uncertainty. It gets everyone on the same side of the table, at many tables. It takes us from complication to simple.

If for funding, branding, or political purposes we need to name official missions, visions, values, or strategies, we can draw from any of our opportunity questions. There is unique power in mission questions, vision questions, values questions, and strategy questions.

So, why do new ventures succeed and fail? Is it because they aren't rigorously goal and plan driven enough?

There is all kind of speculation about why any kind of new ventures fail. New ventures include new businesses and start ups, new products and services, new markets and mergers.

The mythology is that they fail because they have the wrong idea, leadership, talent, plan, spreadsheets, deal sheets, or funding.

The real reason is because of how they go about organizing their uncertainty. Assumptions are their demise.

It's not from a lack of effort. The effort that goes into failed ventures is relatively equal or even greater than that in successful ventures. The difference is in their method which is based in their beliefs about how to best organize uncertainty.

This is easily correctable. All they need is to pivot from goals and plans to opportunity and path questions.

The good news is this does not take new kinds of leadership, talent, or funding. It takes the different language of different approaches. It is a function of discovery. We can inquire and discover our way into the best ventures possible.

How do projects work in a path world?

Whether we talk about personal or shared contexts, projects are classic spaces of uncertainty.

We can decide on all kinds of project requirements, deadlines, resources, and constraints and base them more on assumptions than reality.

No matter how detailed they might be, we also have any number of questions we must and will answer in the life of the project. Some or many of these will challenge or invalidate the reliability of our assumptions.

Uncertainty isn't the starting state of projects. It's the continuous reality of projects. Every question reveals new answers; every answer reveals new questions.

Project uncertainty is best organized by a path method because it bypasses counter-productive dependency on assumptions.

The illusion of project struggle and failure is that these are the result of personal, group, team, leadership, or resources inadequacies. The reality is that projects struggle and fail when we try organizing them with goals and plans rather than paths. Paths move us forward in any project.

Can paths shape how we make decisions or does decision making require a different kind of structure?

On any given day, we make decisions as couples, teams, and groups. Depending on how much uncertainty is involved, we have decisions that can be made quickly and decisions that take more effort and time. Each decision possible is an experience of uncertainty.

What doesn't help decision making is arguing over the assumptions of opinions, expectations, and speculations. Putting a decision off until someone else takes care of it or it resolves itself doesn't help.

Using voting that divides us into majority winners and minority losers doesn't work. Waiting to make the decision once we have no uncertainties doesn't help.

What works is applying a path method to any kind of decision. As we talked about earlier, we make the process simpler and often wiser when we approach uncertainty as experiments.

How do personality differences factor into organizing uncertainty through a path method?

Everyone brings their own vibes to contexts of uncertainty.

There are the continuum of vibes of positivity to negativity, being open to being right, risk friendly to risk averse, self-serving to generous, serious to funny, transparent to opaque, compliant to creative.

A path method doesn't require any change in personality. Everyone can engage and contribute just as they are.

This is because everyone since childhood, whatever their personality, has developed exactly what the process requires.

Everyone knows what uncertainty looks like. Everyone knows how to be curious. Everyone knows the difference between assumption and fact. Everyone knows how to explore things, visualize things, try things, and realize things.

The process makes these abilities accessible. We can engage these no matter what our personalities. Personality is as much a constraint in a path method as shoe size is in cooking.

Because each of us brings a unique chemistry of abilities and perspectives, our shared ability to organize uncertainty is greater together than apart. All it takes is shifts in language.

It would seem logical that navigating uncertainty requires a certain degree of hope. How important is hope?

Hope can imply we have done all we think we can do, and all we have left is waiting with positive anticipation to see what happens. It can also imply waiting for other people or conditions to manage the uncertainty we're experiencing.

Managing by hope can occur when our goals seem out of reach or our plans no longer tenable. We feel stuck and helpless. We regain an illusion of power in blame.

We lack questions or we have no actionable questions. As much as hope might feel good and create an illusion of predictability, it doesn't organize uncertainty.

Whether managing by hope makes sense to our rational mind, it can seem like our only option when we aren't clear how to skillfully organize the uncertainty.

The more we organize uncertainty through a path method, the less we manage by hope.

We're at an interesting inflection point in organizations and communities where there is an emerging kind of leader interested in more engaged members. How can a path method support this direction?

The vast majority of people in organizations and communities worldwide are not engaged. They do not directly participate in together shaping a shared present or future.

A path method provides a way to make this kind of engagement possible.

While formal top leaders still work from goals and plans, people can together work from a path method. The future of shared power, resources, and rewards is in the promise and practice of shared paths.

Goals and plans are by design and definition power-divisive and constraining structures.

Paths are engaging, connecting, and liberating structures.

A path method helps us feel persistently capable and engaged. It imbues and grows a sense of self-efficacy because every step along the way feels possible and successful. We no longer have to assess, compare, or prove our worth.

This is the radical potential of paths. They have the power to finally democratize power. This shift in power creates equity in ways that no amount of lip-service can.

It's the next generation of leaders mastering and facilitating a path method who will catalyze the possible impossible.

Do goals and plans make us personally and collectively ethical? Does a world without goals and plans become less ethical?

Ethics is the domain of empathy. It is interest in knowing and supporting the opportunity and path questions of others. By definition, all paths are ethical paths because we become curious about other peoples questions.

In goals and plans, others are either tools to be used or obstacles to be removed. We can pursue goals and plans with no interest in or commitment to the questions of others. No empathy is required.

This is why companies and governments can pursue goals without empathetic or ethical regard for others.

Paths are intrinsically more empathetic and ethical because in understanding contexts, we become curious about those potentially involved in and impacted by any actions we take along paths.

We naturally engage each other so others can have for themselves what we most want for ourselves.

How do paths relate to communities dedicated to being smart communities?

Our world is a dynamic network of local communities. Our communities have never seen the kinds of challenges and possibilities than those they see today.

Communities now experience types of uncertainty they aren't prepared for.

Nothing in their histories has prepared them for the kinds of uncertainty they see and experience today. None of their predecessors could have even imagined kinds of uncertainty their grandchildren would see.

It's possible for communities to have more wealth and poverty than empathy.

The communities that will survive and thrive on all levels are those that organize uncertainty from the intelligence and ethics of paths.

This is a call for smart communities. It is a call for all companies, institutions, programs, funders, and governments to reinvent and reimagine themselves to be agents of change in the creation of smart communities.

A smart community is a curious, question-based community, continuously exploring and creating new ways of doing anything that matters to the life and growth of the community.

A path method becomes the heart of the smart community.

What about generational differences. Does each generation need to invent and improvise its own approach to organizing uncertainty?

Each generation has its own flavor of uncertainty.

It's not clear if the uncertainty of the younger is more or less prevalent and profound than the uncertainty of the older. Perhaps if anything is true, it is that the uncertainty is different by quality rather than degree.

Why wouldn't the younger and the older have different opportunity questions and different paths? Why wouldn't they have similar opportunity and path questions? Why wouldn't they have opportunity and path questions that are parallel, divergent, and intersect?

Opportunity questions are shaped both by history and the lack of history. The questions of the older are enriched by the lack of history of the younger just as the questions of the younger are enriched by the history of the older.

New questions along paths are inspired in the dialogue between younger and older. In the absence of dialogue, the inconsolable clash and collision of assumptions reign and everyone loses.

A path method keeps the dialogue rich and productive for all.

Is it possible to support others on their paths to organizing uncertainty?

Uncertainty is a reasonable opportunity for shared guidance. Someone trying to organize some kind of uncertainty asks someone else for perspective and insight.

We take turns on each side of this conversation. One day we can be on giving side and the next day on the receiving side.

The supporting person does not necessarily need to be more senior, smarter, or more experienced. Our value is in four simple gifts.

We can listen simply, without judgment. We can offer alternative context views and path options.

We can provide questions that encourage others to listen more deeply to themselves so they can be clear on the truth and beauty of their questions. We can connect them to those who have other gifts distinct from ours.

We can help them think about the optimal timing and sequencing of their questions. We can offer options to consider for other path questions and actions.

We can follow up to assist in lessons learned and progress celebrated. Two indicators of our value is the growth in their self-confidence and creativity.

What about the big questions in life, the ones that spin us into uncertainty? Is it possible to organize these kinds of uncertainty?

Why are we here? What is the meaning of life? What happens after this life? What should we teach our children? What do we need to be prepared for, and how? What should we hope to become? What can we become?

Every big question has more questions alongside them and beneath them than there are answers.

It's OK to not know. It's OK to have more questions than answers if we believe that our questions represent our most honest response to and promise of the present and our relationship to the future.

Although no one can answer them for us, we can use them as catalysts to craft the kinds of paths that lead to meaning and joy.

These are questions that can bring us together rather than divide us apart. They are questions that can call from us our best selves, our best perspectives, and our best efforts to learn our way into the future, the future we most desire to see possible.

What does it mean to navigate everyday uncertainty?

All manner of questions punctuate the everyday cadences of our lives. We struggle and strive to make it through, to eek and seek out the best life we can.

We live in the humility of our limitations, brokenness, and vulnerability. We live in the promise of our yet unknown potential.

Each moment of uncertainty brings us back to realizing the sacredness of our opportunity questions and the sincerity of our paths.

Nothing has more potential than our questions. They expand us to an unpredictable knowing beyond what we expect and assume.

In each expansion we grow, we mature. Our gifts become more accessible. We live a life of contribution more than consumption, abundance more than deficiency.

We become enough, worthy of what calls us. We listen. The listening gives us a wisdom that brings about the kind of delight that realizes dreams. This is the possibility of each fresh moment.

So, where do we ultimately begin?

We can start paths in any aspect of life. It could be where we feel a sense of urgency or where we would like to simply play with it and see how it works. We can start in our personal, work, and civic lives.

We move forward inspired by four truths.

Life is uncertainty.
Uncertainty is an asset.
Assumptions amplify uncertainty.
Curiosity organizes it.

We don't have to wait until we have more certainty. We don't have to wait until we have certain things in order or under control. We don't have to wait until we have more time.

Anytime can be an optimal time to begin our work on paths. We begin anywhere and move gracefully in the direction of opportunities that call our hearts.

From the language of paths, uncertainty empowers the likely improbability of our human potentials.

About the author

Jack's interest as writer informs his work with people in organizations and communities who want to create the best possible world for all. His work began in the late 1970s, inspired by his mentors who were leaders in the human potentials movement.

Supported by the research and writing for two dozen books and thousands of blog posts and articles, Jack continues to work across industries and geographies with entrepreneurs and Fortune 500s, aboriginal tribal leaders and executive teams, scientists and educators, organic farmers and tech innovators, funders and investors, nonprofits and grass roots groups, government leaders and doctors, designers and innovators.

With a graduate degree in psychology from Goddard College in Vermont, Jack's teaching portfolio includes storytelling at Harvard Kennedy School, research branding at UC

Berkeley, and executive leadership at Kent State University.

Jack is co-founder and partner with Thrive At Work. For more about Jack, visit NuanceWorks.com

Gratitude

All of my books have emerged from and grown in conversation.

Thanks to cherished friends and some of the wisest souls on the planet: Doug Craver, Jen Margolis, Doug Heuer, Mandy Varley, Scott Anderson, Jim Kulma, and Gary Schoeniger.

For book orders, visit PathMethod.co

Made in the
USA
Lexington, KY